NEW EDITION

THE PRESIDENT'S CABINET
And How It Grew

by Nancy Winslow Parker
with an Introduction by the Honorable Dean Rusk

HarperCollins Publishers

The author wishes to thank the following U.S. Government workers and private citizens for the help they have given her in the preparation of this book: Congressman Bill Green, 15th District New York • Ann Sauerman and Beth Myers in Congressman Green's Office • Rex W. Scouten, Curator, The White House • Honor Willson, Office of Cabinet Affairs, The White House • Chris Vein, Management and Administration, The White House • Richard M. Hadsell, General Services Administration • The Library of Congress, Congressional Research Service • The Lyndon Baines Johnson Library • Tom Hughes, Office of Public Affairs, United States Department of the Interior • Linda L. Kay, Alumnae Director, Mills College, California • Mary D. Merrill, Peggy L. Pierce, and Mrs. Nicholson, descendants of Norman J. Colman, first Secretary of Agriculture.

Library of Congress Cataloging-in-Publication Data
Parker, Nancy Winslow.
    The president's cabinet and how it grew / by Nancy Winslow Parker ; with an introduction by Dean Rusk. — New ed.
        p.   cm.
    Summary: Outlines the purpose and historical development of the President's cabinet, and explains the functions of each cabinet post.
    ISBN 0-06-021617-4.—ISBN 0-06-021618-2 (lib. bdg.)
    1. Cabinet officers — United States—Juvenile literature.
[1. Cabinet officers.]   I. Title.
JK611.P37   1991   89-70851
353.04—dc20   CIP
                                                AC

1 2 3 4 5 6 7 8 9 10
New Edition

To Mills College,
and the Class of '52

The United States has the most complicated constitutional
and political system to be found anywhere in the world. Our
Founding Fathers deliberately made it that way to protect our
individual liberties from those who govern. Foreigners find it
very hard to understand our constitutional system—and so do
many of us Americans. I welcome what Nancy Winslow Parker
has done in this book; she tells about the President's Cabinet
accurately, clearly—and with a smile.

Dean Rusk
54th Secretary of State

This is not the President's Cabinet.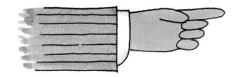

This is the President's Cabinet . . .

SEC. OF STATE

SEC. OF TREASURY

SEC. OF DEFENSE

ATTORNEY GENERAL

SEC. OF INTERIOR

SEC. OF AGRICULTURE

SEC. OF COMMERCE

SEC. OF LABOR

SEC. OF HEALTH
AND HUMAN SERVICES

SEC. OF HOUSING
AND URBAN DEVELOPMENT

SEC. OF TRANSPORTATION

SEC. OF ENERGY

SEC. OF EDUCATION

SEC. OF VETERANS AFFAIRS

SEC. OF THE ENVIRONMENT

…fifteen men and women chosen by the President of the United States to give advice and help run the executive branch of the federal government.

The President is our Chief Executive. Under the Constitution, he alone has the power to decide on national policy and to administer all the laws passed by Congress—the House of Representatives and the Senate. No law, however, says that the President must have a Cabinet. The Constitution says only that the President "may require the opinion, in writing, of the principal officer in each of the executive departments, upon any subject relating to the duties of their respective offices." The President does not have to ask for this advice, and, when it is given, he does not have to take it.

The President's Cabinet is not a formal executive organization. It is for observation only. No votes are taken at Cabinet meetings, and minutes are not kept. Notes, memos, and personal diaries are history's source for information on what was said in Cabinet meetings.

Nevertheless, the President has a group of official advisors, because no one person can know about everything that is going on in the nation. Any leader needs reliable counselors to provide information and advice. This has been true since prehistoric people first huddled around council fires in their tents and caves.

Each President chooses the members of his Cabinet with the "advice and consent" of the Senate, but they serve at the President's pleasure and can be fired at any time. They are picked for their knowledge, their experience, their special talents, or their general wisdom. They may be old and trusted friends, sometimes even relatives. They can be rich or poor, thinkers or doers—farmers, bankers, diplomats, scientists, or politicians. They come from all parts of the United States. When the President leaves office, his entire Cabinet resigns, and the new President picks his own Cabinet—sometimes retaining or reassigning the previous Cabinet members.

They meet weekly around a big mahogany table in the Cabinet Room next to the President's Oval Office in the West Wing of the White House. This beautiful room faces the Rose Garden and is furnished with draperies, brass chandeliers, and chairs copied from late-eighteenth-century American designs. A portrait of Abraham Lincoln hangs over the fireplace at one end of the room.

The word "cabinet," like many other American terms, came from eighteenth-century England, where a private meeting room was often called a cabinet. James Madison first used the word to refer to the President's advisors.

There haven't always been fifteen members of the Cabinet. As our country grew and changed, particular Presidents added Cabinet members to meet special needs. The latest addition is the Secretary of the Environment. He will be seated to the right of the Secretary of Veterans Affairs, at the end of the table; the Chief of Staff will move to the other end of the table, next to the U.S. Trade Representative.

The President, Cabinet Members, and Key Advisors

George Washington's Cabinet · 1789

In 1789, when the Constitution went into effect, Congress passed laws creating the first three Executive Departments of the new government: State, Treasury, and War. The head of each department was to be called the Secretary.

George Washington, the first president, picked a rich landowner and fellow Virginian, Thomas Jefferson, to be the first Secretary of State, with many duties both at home and abroad. Alexander Hamilton, a New Yorker, became Secretary of the Treasury, in charge of collecting taxes, creating a banking system, issuing money, and printing postage stamps. The Secretary of War was Henry Knox of Massachusetts, who had been a general in the Revolutionary War. Then, since the first President would also need legal advice, Congress created the office of Attorney General, and Washington appointed a second Virginian, his close friend Edmund Randolph, to fill the job. The Attorney General was considered a Cabinet member from the start, though he did not become head of a department—the Justice Department—until after the Civil War.

In the beginning, Washington consulted with his Cabinet members one at a time, occasionally asking for written opinions. But soon they all met together regularly, probably in Washington's home at 3 Cherry Street in New York City, the first capital of the United States after the Constitution was ratified. In 1790, Philadelphia became the temporary capital. In 1800, the government moved to Washington, D.C., to a site chosen by George Washington.

HENRY KNOX
1st Secretary of War

ALEXANDER HAMILTON
1st Secretary of the Treasury

THOMAS JEFFERSON
1st Secretary of State

EDMUND RANDOLPH
1st Attorney General

11

BENJAMIN STODDERT
1st Secretary of the Navy

John Adams's Cabinet · 1798

The second President managed nicely at first with a four-man Cabinet. He had even invited Washington's entire Cabinet to stay on at the start of his term. Then, in 1798, there was trouble on the high seas. Both the British and French navies began to threaten American merchant ships. And the Barbary pirates off the coast of Africa were harassing our ships and sailors. We needed a fighting fleet, and so Congress created a separate Department of the Navy. President John Adams chose Benjamin Stoddert of Maryland, who had served in the Revolutionary War, to be its first Secretary. Stoddert's job was to build a U.S. Navy able to protect American ships at sea, to safeguard the lives of American seamen, and to defend our shores. Secretary Stoddert also established the U.S. Marine Corps.

During Adams's term, the Cabinet probably met in the President's office, on the second floor of the new White House in Washington, D.C.

Andrew Jackson's Cabinet · 1829

Andrew Jackson, the seventh President of the United States, was from the frontier state of Tennessee. He was so hot-tempered that he once called for the resignation of his entire Cabinet when their conduct displeased him. For almost two years, Jackson stopped holding Cabinet meetings and relied instead on the advice of an informal group of political cronies who came to be called "The Kitchen Cabinet." Before Jackson's time, those who were chosen to be Cabinet members were considered likely future candidates for President. But Jackson refused to consider anyone for a Cabinet post if the man had the slightest ambition to be President. In 1829 he raised the job of Postmaster General to Cabinet rank and appointed an old political friend, William T. Barry, of Kentucky, to the job. Until then the Post Office had been under the Treasury Department. By promoting the Postmaster General to Cabinet rank, Jackson could control the appointing of Post Office jobs, making sure they went to his political friends as rewards for their support. And until 1970, the job of Postmaster General was always given to a loyal worker in the President's own party.

WILLIAM T. BARRY
1st Postmaster General

THOMAS EWING
1st Secretary of the Interior

Zachary Taylor's Cabinet · 1849

"Old Rough and Ready" was the nickname of our twelfth President, an Army general who commanded U.S. troops during the Mexican War. He took office at a time when large numbers of Americans were moving westward to settle new territories. The previous President, James Polk, had, on his very last day in office, signed into law a congressional bill establishing a Department of the Interior. It would not only be in charge of millions of acres of new government land acquired during the preceding half century, but also be responsible for the Indians who lived on the land.

President Taylor appointed Thomas Ewing of Ohio to be its first Secretary. The Department was also to supervise the use of natural and mineral resources on public lands, to take a census every ten years, and to protect inventors by issuing patents on their inventions.

Grover Cleveland's Cabinet · 1889

Answering the clamor from farmers, Grover Cleveland, the twenty-second President, raised the Department of Agriculture to Cabinet rank. He appointed Norman J. Colman of Missouri, a farm journalist and lawyer, as its first Secretary. The farmers' unrest had started during Abraham Lincoln's first term as President. A series of poor harvests and marketing problems in various parts of the country made farmers want to have someone in the executive branch who knew about wheat and corn, pigs and cows, flooding and droughts. The first Department of Agriculture, formed in 1862, had not been given Cabinet rank. It took twenty-seven more years before Agriculture became a full-fledged executive department. The new Secretary Colman was in charge of letting the farmers know about the latest developments in soil conservation, crop rotation, planting techniques, and livestock breeding. He also told the President what the farmers were thinking. As the nation grew, the President had to know how citizens with various interests were affected by government policies.

Cleveland's eight Cabinet members met with him in the Treaty Room on the second floor of the White House.

NORMAN J. COLMAN
1st Secretary of Agriculture

15

Theodore Roosevelt's Cabinet · 1903

A champion of the rights of "the little man," Theodore Roosevelt, the twenty-sixth President, was in office during the coal strike of 1902, when anthracite miners refused to work. Their grievances were poor pay, long hours, wretched working conditions, and the mine owners' refusal to recognize their union. By this time, many businesses had grown so big and powerful that they could force workers to accept unsafe and unpleasant working conditions—or keep them from having jobs at all. Also, the prosperity of the country was coming to depend more and more on the productivity and management of big business. It was important that there be a government agency to represent not only the workers, but the business interests of the nation. So in 1903 a joint Department of Commerce and Labor was established. President Roosevelt appointed George B. Cortelyou, a big businessman from New York, as the first Secretary. It was his job to represent the interests of both the businessmen and laborers in all kinds of industry. He was also ordered to investigate big corporations and examine the agreements they made with one another.

It was Roosevelt's Cabinet that first met in the present-day Cabinet Room of the White House.

GEORGE B. CORTELYOU
1st Secretary of Commerce and Labor

Woodrow Wilson's Cabinet · 1913

Long, hard work by various labor organizations led to the creation of a separate Department of Labor in 1913. By this time the United States had clearly changed from a country of farmers and small businessmen into an industrial society dependent on hired labor. These workers included not only American men and women, but thousands of immigrants who came here from Europe eager to find work in the "land of opportunity." Woodrow Wilson, the twenty-eighth President, appointed William B. Wilson from Pennsylvania, a major coal-producing state, to be the first Secretary of Labor. William Cox Redfield of New York, a manufacturer and congressman, became the first Secretary of the now separate Commerce Department. It was the job of the new Labor Department to help initiate and then administer fair laws regulating hours, pay, and conditions of labor for all workers—including children, who were then underpaid and overworked by many mill and factory owners. The Secretary of Commerce remained to help promote American business at home and in foreign markets, too.

The Secretary of Labor became the first Cabinet position to be held by a woman, when in 1933 President Franklin Delano Roosevelt appointed Frances Perkins of New York to be the fourth Secretary of Labor.

WILLIAM B. WILSON
1st Secretary of Labor

WILLIAM COX REDFIELD
1st Secretary of Commerce

Harry S Truman's Cabinet · 1947

When Harry Truman succeeded Franklin D. Roosevelt as the thirty-third President, the Cabinet had not undergone any changes in more than thirty years. After World War II, with our armed forces in various parts of the world, it was no longer sensible to divide military responsibilities between rival War and Navy Departments. The Air Corps had grown so important that it, too, needed a separate Department. So in 1947 Congress created the Department of Defense to supervise the Departments of the Army, the Navy, and the Air Force. The Marine Corps continued under the Department of the Navy. The Department of War was abolished. President Truman appointed Secretary of the Navy James V. Forrestal of New York to be the first Secretary of Defense. He became the supervisor not only of all the armed forces, but of the many thousands of civilian workers in the Department as well. Because the Defense job is so big and complex, it is usually given to an executive of a large corporation. Truman called his Cabinet "a board of directors appointed by the President to help him carry out the policies of government."

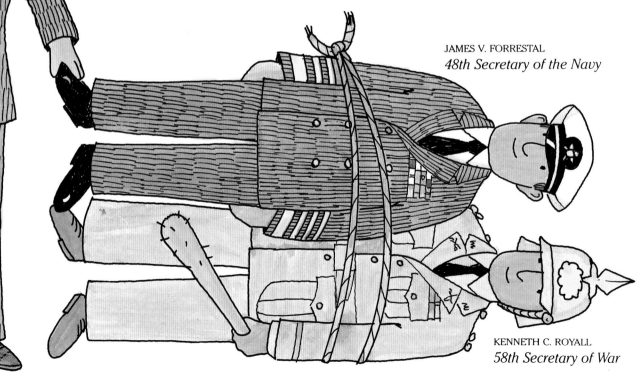

JAMES V. FORRESTAL
1st Secretary of Defense

JAMES V. FORRESTAL
48th Secretary of the Navy

KENNETH C. ROYALL
58th Secretary of War

Dwight D. Eisenhower's Cabinet · 1953

By the early fifties, our country had become increasingly aware of the special needs of its citizens in the areas of health, education, and welfare. Though Americans have always been self-reliant, as our society grew more industrialized, families and friends were scattered and less able to help one another. A number of separate agencies had been created over the years to provide assistance: the Public Health Service, the Office of Education, the Food and Drug Administration, the National Institutes of Health, the Social Security Administration, and the Welfare Administration. In 1953 all these agencies were put together in one new Department of Health, Education and Welfare (H.E.W.). Dwight D. Eisenhower, our thirty-fourth President, appointed Oveta Culp Hobby of Texas, the former commander of the Women's Army Corps, to be its first Secretary. The Constitution's promise to the American people, "to promote the General Welfare...," was to be carried out through H.E.W.'s programs on aging, Native Americans, family assistance, children and youth, persons living in rural areas, and the handicapped.

OVETA CULP HOBBY
1st Secretary of Health, Education and Welfare

ROBERT C. WEAVER
*1st Secretary of Housing
and Urban Development*

Ever since World War I, small sums of money had been spent by the federal government to provide housing, loans for home buying, and help for slum clearance and urban development. But as our cities grew larger, the problems of overcrowding grew, too. In 1965 Lyndon B. Johnson, our thirty-sixth President, signed a bill creating the Department of Housing and Urban Development (H.U.D.), so that more attention could be paid to the special problems of big cities. He named Robert C. Weaver from the District of Columbia to be its first Secretary. Weaver was the first black person to serve in the Cabinet.

Two years later, President Johnson signed another congressional bill, this time creating a Department of Transportation. Again, because of the country's amazing growth, it had become necessary to have a national policy that would help provide safe and adequate transportation—by train, bus, car, or plane—to all parts of the nation. Alan S. Boyd of Florida was the first Secretary of Transportation.

ALAN S. BOYD
1st Secretary of Transportation

Richard M. Nixon's Cabinet · 1970

The Cabinet today is minus one old-timer, the Postmaster General. By the late 1960s the Post Office Department had become the sixth-largest business in the United States, handling some 90 billion pieces of mail per year and employing more than 700,000 postal workers. But despite its size and importance, the Post Office Department was losing more and more money every year. This prompted Richard Nixon, the thirty-seventh President, and the Congress to reorganize it in 1970 as the U.S. Postal Service. It became a separate government corporation to be run like any other big business—for profit, free from political pressures to change local postmasters with each new Presidential administration. Another result of the reorganization was that, in 1973, the Postmaster General lost his seat in the Cabinet.

SHIRLEY M. HUFSTEDLER
1st Secretary of Education

PATRICIA ROBERTS HARRIS
*1st Secretary of Health
and Human Services*

JAMES R. SCHLESINGER
1st Secretary of Energy

22

Jimmy Carter's Cabinet · 1977, 1979

At the time Jimmy Carter became the thirty-ninth President, the whole world was worried about the high price of oil and concerned that the great industrial nations were using too much gasoline, electricity, and natural gas. A worldwide energy crisis was feared. The President asked Congress to establish a Department of Energy to plan sound energy conservation policies for private citizens and industry. In 1977 President Carter chose James R. Schlesinger of Virginia to be the new Department's first Secretary.

Two years later, President Carter reorganized the Department of Health, Education and Welfare. The "Education" part became the Department of Education, with Judge Shirley M. Hufstedler of California as its first Secretary. Since 1908 nearly 130 pieces of legislation had been introduced in Congress proposing a Department of Education. Finally, in 1979, Congress passed the act creating the Department of Education to address the nation's educational problems—a decline in the quality of education, a high rate of school dropouts, young people with no skills to hold down jobs, and demands from workers to retrain in new fields.

With the elimination of "Education" from H.E.W., and "Welfare" renamed "Human Services," a new Department was born—Health and Human Services (H.H.S.), with an enormous budget of almost $200 billion annually. Only two organizational entities on earth had larger budgets than H.H.S. in 1979—the government of the United States and the government of the Soviet Union. President Carter appointed Patricia Roberts Harris, a black woman from the District of Columbia and a former Secretary of H.U.D., as the first Secretary.

George Bush's Cabinet · 1989, 1990

In 1988, there were 27,359,000 veterans in civilian life in the United States, from the two who had served in the Spanish-American War to the 8,277,000 from the Vietnam Era. It was to represent this very large group of people that President Reagan, in his last months in office, signed a congressional bill elevating the Veterans Administration to Cabinet rank. The bill was clearly a political move in an election year, "a gesture towards an important group of people," a senior White House official said. The Veterans Administration is fifty-eight years old. It provides benefits to veterans and their families, and medical treatment to three million veterans a year. The new Department of Veterans Affairs (D.V.A.) was not officially established until March 1989, so President Bush was entitled to name its first Secretary. He chose his good friend Edward J. Derwinski, from Illinois, a former congressman, World War II veteran, and State Department official.

In early 1990, legislation was introduced in Congress to elevate the Environmental Protection Agency (E.P.A.) to a Cabinet Department. This was a response to the serious environmental hazards facing Americans—pollution of the air we breathe, the water we drink, and the food we eat. Congress was expected to pass the bill by the end of the year. Being in the President's Cabinet will give the Secretary of the Environment more power to clean up America and the chance to work with other nations on the world problems of global warming, ocean dumping, and toxic wastes.

WILLIAM REILLY
1st Secretary of the Environment

24

Others Who Attend Cabinet Meetings

The President may also grant "Cabinet-level rank" to other advisors, allowing them to participate in cabinet meetings. In 1961, President John F. Kennedy gave the U.S. Representative to the United Nations Cabinet-level rank in his administration. By doing so, he stressed the importance of the United Nations, and gave the Ambassador, Adlai E. Stevenson, a greater voice in foreign policy than any of his predecessors had had.

The ambassadorship to the United Nations is a State Department post under the supervision of the Secretary of State. In 1988, President-elect George Bush removed the United Nations Ambassador from Cabinet-level rank, preferring to have him less visible in internal policy-making debates. It was also thought that the Ambassador's presence in Cabinet meetings would dilute the Secretary of State's authority and unbalance the Cabinet with two people from the State Department.

In addition to the fifteen Secretaries, Bush's Cabinet includes three Executive Officers. They are:

1. The White House Chief of Staff;
2. The U.S. Trade Representative;
3. The Director of the Office of Management and Budget (OMB)

Staff aides of the Cabinet attend meetings and sit in chairs at the sides of the Cabinet Room. In some administrations, the First Lady has sat in back of the President.

During the 19th century, Vice Presidents sat in on Cabinet meetings only occasionally. In 1921, President Warren Harding invited Vice President Calvin Coolidge to be a regular attendant. Today, the Vice President attends every meeting.

The Secretaries and Their Departments

When the members of the President's Cabinet are not sitting in the Cabinet Room giving the President advice and discussing the affairs of the nation—from the problems of homeless people and drug addiction in the United States to international terrorism and arms reductions in Europe—they are running their own executive departments from offices in Washington, D.C. Some offices are very large—like the Defense Department's Pentagon, the largest office building in the world, with 25,965 employees; or the Department of Education's offices on Maryland Avenue, where 3,294 people work. Each Department is still in charge of many of the things it was originally entrusted to do. Some responsibilities, however, have been shifted—such as taking the census, which began as a duty of the Department of the Interior and is now handled by the Department of Commerce. The Peace Corps, which used to be part of the State Department, was turned into an independent agency in 1977.

The policies set by the president, with the help of his Cabinet members and their Departments, often result in new laws and national goals that affect almost every aspect of American life today.

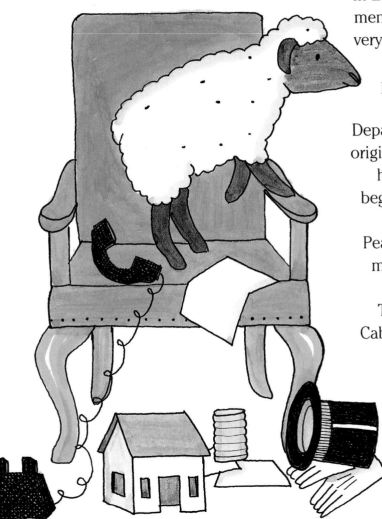

The Secretary of State

has the most important job in the Cabinet—President Eisenhower once called it "the greatest and most important job in the world." He is the first-ranking member of the Cabinet and a member of the National Security Council. The Secretary of State recommends foreign policy and keeps the President informed about what is happening at all times in every part of the world. He travels widely, talking with prime ministers, monarchs, and other heads of state to negotiate terms for various government agreements and to promote good relations with foreign countries. He is in charge of all U.S. diplomats and foreign-service officers assigned to embassies, consulates, and other missions all over the world, including the U.S. Mission to the United Nations in New York. When he is in Washington, he meets with State Department specialists and foreign diplomats stationed in this country. The State Department issues passports—and provides protection—to American citizens who travel abroad, for either business or pleasure. It also operates refugee programs overseas for the relief and repatriation of refugees and selects refugees to come to the United States.

The Secretary of the Treasury

is in charge of everything to do with money. He recommends the economic policy the United States should follow. His Department supervises the chartering of banks and watches over the national banking system. It collects federal income taxes, export and import duties, and other special taxes. The Bureau of the Mint, which manufactures and distributes U.S. coins, comes under the Secretary, as does the Bureau of Engraving and Printing, which designs and produces paper money, savings bonds, and postage stamps. And the Secret Service, of all things, answers to the Secretary of the Treasury. Organized in 1865 to arrest counterfeiters, forgers, smugglers, and other criminals out to cheat the federal government, the Secret Service began the job of protecting the President in 1901, after the assassination of President McKinley. Until the Federal Bureau of Investigation—the F.B.I.—was organized under the Justice Department in 1908, the Secret Service was the main law-enforcement agency of the government.

The Secretary of Defense

is responsible for keeping the United States strong enough militarily to defend itself against any enemy. The Secretary, who has always been a civilian, is in charge of buying planes, tanks, guns, and missiles from private industry for the armed forces, paying military personnel, and taking care of their health. His Department spends more than one quarter of the money in the national budget—much more than any other Department. Under the President, who is Commander in Chief, the Secretary directs the Army, Navy, and Air Force Departments, the Joint Chiefs of Staff who provide military advice, and other defense agencies. From the Department's Pentagon offices, the Secretary directs 2.2 million men and women on active duty, 1.7 million reserves, and 1.2 million civilian employees. Finally, the Secretary has control over the schools where officers are trained: the U.S. Military Academy, the U.S. Naval Academy, and the U.S. Air Force Academy.

The Attorney General

is the chief lawyer for the United States and is in charge of the Justice Department. His job includes detecting and prosecuting all violators of federal law: spies, traitors, kidnappers, thieves who transport stolen goods across state lines, and other criminals. With the help of many U.S. Attorneys, he represents the government in civil and criminal courts. When a case is exceptionally important, he appears before the Supreme Court. He is responsible for the Federal Bureau of Investigation, the nation's chief law-enforcement agency, and the Drug Enforcement Administration. He directs all federal prisons—including training schools for juvenile delinquents. The Department's Immigration and Naturalization Service registers all aliens entering the United States and examines anyone applying for citizenship. The enforcement of the clean air and water laws falls to the Attorney General.

The Secretary of the Interior

is the chief guardian of the nation's natural resources. His Department supervises more than 500 million acres of government land and operates more than 340 national parks and other historic and recreational places for everyone to enjoy. These range from the 2.2-million-acre Yellowstone National Park in Wyoming to the home of Martin Van Buren, the eighth President of the United States, in Kinderhook, New York. The welfare of some 864,500 American Indians living on or adjacent to reservations totaling 53 million acres of land, is also his responsibility. The Department looks after the fish and wildlife in our rivers and forests, leases offshore drilling rights to oil companies, and enforces safety regulations in mines. It operates some 300 dams and 250 reservoirs and hundreds of miles of canals, pipelines, and tunnels to benefit the western United States. Also, it operates 51 hydroelectric plants that supply electricity to 51 million people. The sale of this power returns $675 million to the federal treasury. The Department also helps to administer or promote various island territories—Guam, American Samoa, the U.S. Virgin Islands, the Northern Marianas, and the Republic of Palau. It oversees federal programs to the Marshall Islands and Micronesia.

The Secretary of Agriculture

is usually a person from one of the large farm states of the Middle West. He is the Cabinet member most involved in Americans' day-to-day living. His job is to help farmers grow better crops and ranchers to breed healthier animals. By keeping up with worldwide agricultural developments, the Department can advise farmers about how best to conserve the soil, prevent erosion, and plant crops that will sell at good prices. To protect farmers against natural disasters and overproduction, the Department also operates insurance and price-support programs. And to protect the consumer, the Department inspects meat, poultry, and eggs to make sure they are wholesome. Hundreds of thousands of schoolchildren receive low-cost or free milk and lunches through this Department, which also administers the food-stamp program for low-income families. The Forest Service, which switched from the Department of the Interior to the Department of Agriculture in 1905, manages national forests and grasslands for recreation, beauty, wildlife habitat, and water supply—for the people's needs today and in the future.

The Secretary of Commerce

promotes economic development and technological improvements so that our nation will produce more and better goods to sell at home and abroad. His Department designs programs to support our free-enterprise system, offering aid and advice to many businesses, including minority businesses. By granting inventors patents on their inventions, the Department makes sure that creative work is protected. It is the Secretary's responsibility to take the census every ten years and to provide social and economic statistics for business and government planners. Also under his supervision are the National Bureau of Standards, which sets out rules for measurements, and the National Oceanic and Atmospheric Administration, which draws maps and navigational charts and provides the National Weather Service's daily forecasts. In 1978 the National Telecommunications and Information Administration (NTIA) was created by the Department to be the President's advisor on the way we transmit information, from TV and radio to satellite and radar. In 1982 the Department began encouraging travel and tourism in the United States by Americans and foreign travelers.

The Secretary of Labor

represents the interests of working men and women—on the job and when they are unemployed. It is her task to see that everyone who wants work can find a job and be paid a fair wage. In times of depression or economic change, the Department works to create new public service jobs and provide job training for those who are unemployed. When someone loses a job, the Department helps the state to pay unemployment compensation, and when immigrants arrive, it tries to find them jobs without causing U.S.-born workers to lose theirs. Like the Department of Commerce, this Department also collects statistics, hoping to discover what future job needs will be. It works to protect the rights of all workers by proposing new labor laws whenever they are needed.

The Secretary of Health and Human Services

is the Cabinet member most concerned with human needs from the newborn baby's to the oldest citizen's. He supervises many federal medical care programs. His Department sponsors research on cancer, mental health, arthritis, and AIDS; and drug, alcohol, and tobacco addiction. Working with state and local governments, it helps control epidemics and communicable diseases, and deals with toxic substances in the environment. Through the Food and Drug Administration, the Department tries to ensure that the foods we eat and the drugs we take are safe and accurately labeled. Several services are devoted to the sound development of the nation's children, including their health and support in low-income families, and prevention of their abuse and neglect. The Secretary supervises the biggest insurance program in the world—the Social Security Administration—which pays out monthly benefits to retired or disabled workers. H.H.S. represents the concerns of Native Americans (American Indians, Alaskan Natives, and Native Hawaiians), and serves as liaison with other federal agencies on Native American affairs. The Department also runs programs to help the old, the needy, and the handicapped.

The Secretary of Housing and Urban Development

tries to ensure that every American family has a decent place to live in a safe and healthful community. The Secretary and his assistants study the problems of American cities and try to find new ways for people to live and work comfortably together. His Department helps people borrow money to buy their own homes, or gives rental assistance to people who cannot afford to buy. It takes steps to ensure that all races and ages have equal access to all housing. The Department gives federal funds to cities to clear slums, redevelop neglected areas, and provide low- and middle-income housing. States, local governments, and developers can receive special financial and technical help to plan and build city and rural communities. H.U.D. encourages research into the use of new building materials. Broken-down buildings are transferred to "homesteaders" to fix up and live in. All the building up and tearing down of housing must meet federal standards for the environment, and care must be taken not to disrupt archaeology, historic preservation, wetlands, and endangered species.

The Secretary of Transportation

tries to provide safe, fast, and inexpensive ways for people to travel within and between cities, and for industry to send its products to markets all over the country by rail or air or truck. He must also see that the oil and gas pipelines are operating safely. To help handle this huge job, the Secretary has the Federal Aviation Administration to watch over the operation of air traffic, and to test planes, pilots, and air and ground crews to make sure they meet government standards. The Secretary supervises interstate highway construction, and his Department can give money to states to improve their roads. It also establishes and enforces safety standards for cars and trains. The Secretary directs the U.S. Coast Guard, which helps guarantee safe passage and navigational assistance to ships and boats in lakes and rivers, on the St. Lawrence Seaway, and even in waters off our coasts. The Coast Guard helps to catch drug traffickers and smugglers. In time of war, the Coast Guard functions as a service of the Navy.

The Secretary of Energy

has the difficult job of watching over this country's precious energy resources and regulating their use. He must balance energy use, safety, and the environment. His Department is involved in research and development of all kinds of energy—fossil fuels (coal, petroleum, and gas), renewable fuels (solar, biomass, wind, geothermal, alcohol), and nuclear fuels. It sells hydroelectric and nuclear energy to civilians, and works at energy conservation. It can ask Congress to raise taxes on gasoline or crude oil, to add a special tax on automobiles that use too much gasoline, and to set higher taxes on the use of oil and natural gas by public utilities and big industrial companies. The Secretary's most important task today is to modernize and restore the environment at seventeen main nuclear weapons plants which the Department operates, a job that Congress says may take a hundred years and $100 to $200 billion. The nuclear waste and spent nuclear fuel from these plants must be disposed of in a method safe to civilians and to the environment.

The Secretary of Education

has the job of helping to educate almost everyone—students, parents, migrant workers, Native Americans, and the handicapped—about everything from alcoholism to the environment. For those who don't understand English, the predominant language of the United States, the Department funds bilingual teachers and minority language classes. In addition to the educational programs of the former H.E.W., the Department has taken over from Defense the running of the overseas schools; from Agriculture its graduate schools; from Justice the law-enforcement education programs; from H.U.D. the college housing loans; and from the National Science Foundation its science education programs. The Secretary is responsible for four federally funded corporations—the American Printing House for the Blind, Gallaudet University (for the deaf), Howard University (predominantly black students), the National Technical Institute for the Deaf, and Rochester Institute of Technology (for the deaf).

The Secretary of Veterans Affairs

is in charge of providing benefits to veterans of American wars and their families. He runs the veterans' hospitals, pays benefits, issues insurance, and erects memorials. His Department provides medical care to 3 million vets. It manages 172 hospitals and 112 nursing homes in the United States, Puerto Rico, and the Republic of the Philippines. The Secretary works to find jobs for and train veterans, both able-bodied and disabled. The children of veterans disabled in the Korean and Vietnam wars receive educational assistance from the D.V.A. Veterans also receive pensions, compensation for wounds, and home loans. Their families receive death benefits. The Department manages 112 cemeteries, among them Arlington National Cemetery in Alexandria, Virginia, where President John F. Kennedy, a former Navy officer, is buried. Any veteran, from any war, including the Revolutionary War, is entitled to a tombstone from D.V.A.

The Secretary of the Environment

protects and enhances the environment today and for future generations. His Department carries on the mission of the E.P.A.: "to control and abate pollution in the areas of air, water, solid waste, pesticides, radiation and toxic substances." The Secretary directs his department to attack pollution in cooperation with state and local governments. The Department controls pollution by four methods. Its office of Research and Development sends the latest methods of pollution control to the Department's ten regional offices for dissemination among state and local governments. The Department sets strict standards for the manufacture of goods, from plastic toys to automobiles. Department agents monitor belching smokestacks and smelly factories. And the Department will set fines or punishments, under environmental laws enacted by Congress, for any company that does not pass inspection. The goal of everyone in the Department, from the Director of the Office of Drinking Water to the Director of the Office of Underground Storage Tanks, is for the American citizen to enjoy a livable environment. As the new Department is being formed, it may pick up a wide range of new duties, covering health, natural resources, farming, and manufacture, formerly performed by other Departments.

UNITED STATES BOUNDARIES AND TERRITORIES at the time of

George Washington's Cabinet · 1789

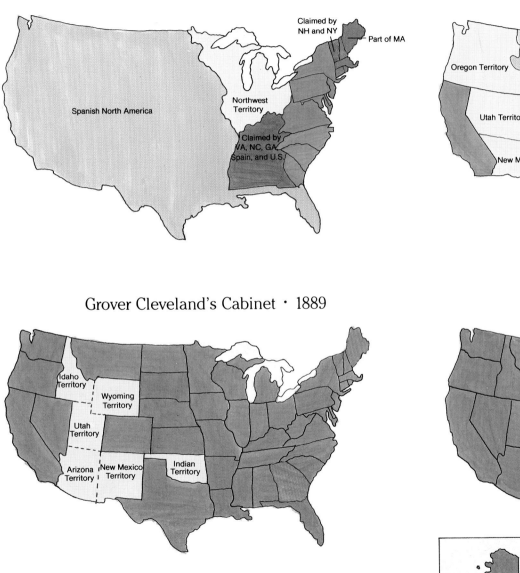

Claimed by
NH and NY

Part of MA

Spanish North America

Northwest
Territory

Claimed by
VA, NC, GA,
Spain, and U.S.

Zachary Taylor's Cabinet · 1850

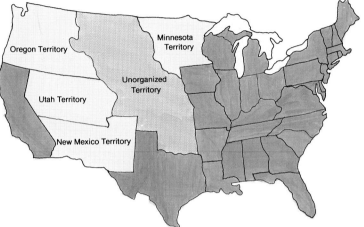

Oregon Territory

Minnesota
Territory

Unorganized
Territory

Utah Territory

New Mexico Territory

Grover Cleveland's Cabinet · 1889

Idaho
Territory

Wyoming
Territory

Utah
Territory

Arizona
Territory

New Mexico
Territory

Indian
Territory

George Bush's Cabinet · 1989

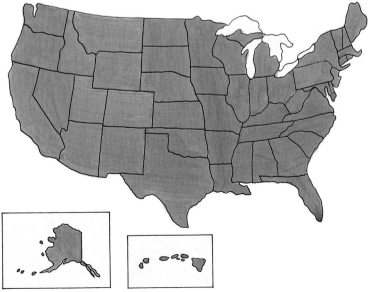

PRESIDENT	TERM OF OFFICE	CABINET CHANGE
1. George Washington	1789–1797	Created Secretaries of State, Treasury, War, and Attorney General
2. John Adams	1797–1801	Added Secretary of Navy
3. Thomas Jefferson	1801–1809	
4. James Madison	1809–1817	
5. James Monroe	1817–1825	
6. John Quincy Adams	1825–1829	
7. Andrew Jackson	1829–1837	Added Postmaster General
8. Martin Van Buren	1837–1841	
9. William Henry Harrison	1841	
10. John Tyler	1841–1845	
11. James K. Polk	1845–1849	
12. Zachary Taylor	1849–1850	Added Secretary of Interior
13. Millard Fillmore	1850–1853	
14. Franklin Pierce	1853–1857	
15. James Buchanan	1857–1861	
16. Abraham Lincoln	1861–1865	
17. Andrew Johnson	1865–1869	
18. Ulysses S. Grant	1869–1877	
19. Rutherford B. Hayes	1877–1881	
20. James A. Garfield	1881	
21. Chester A. Arthur	1881–1885	
22. Grover Cleveland	1885–1889	Added Secretary of Agriculture
23. Benjamin Harrison	1889–1893	
24. Grover Cleveland	1893–1897	
25. William McKinley	1897–1901	
26. Theodore Roosevelt	1901–1909	Added Secretary of Commerce and Labor

PRESIDENT	TERM OF OFFICE	CABINET CHANGE
27. William H. Taft	1909–1913	
28. Woodrow Wilson	1913–1921	Divided Department of Commerce and Labor into Department of Commerce, Department of Labor
29. Warren Harding	1921–1923	
30. Calvin Coolidge	1923–1929	
31. Herbert Hoover	1929–1933	
32. Franklin D. Roosevelt	1933–1945	
33. Harry S Truman	1945–1953	Combined War Department and Department of Navy into Department of Defense
34. Dwight D. Eisenhower	1953–1961	Added Department of Health, Education and Welfare (H.E.W.)
35. John F. Kennedy	1961–1963	
36. Lyndon B. Johnson	1963–1969	Added Departments of Housing and Urban Development (H.U.D.) and Transportation Deleted Postmaster General
37. Richard M. Nixon	1969–1974	
38. Gerald R. Ford	1974–1977	
39. Jimmy Carter	1977–1981	Divided H.E.W. into Departments of Education and Health and Human Services (H.H.S.); added Department of Energy
40. Ronald Reagan	1981–1989	Added Department of Veterans Affairs (D.V.A.)
41. George Bush	1989–	Added Department of Environment

1991 (ESTIMATE) CABINET DEPARTMENT OUTLAYS* (in millions of dollars)

1. Defense (military and civil) — 317,662
2. Treasury — 254,928
3. Health and Human Services — 204,082
   - Social Security — 260,089
4. Agriculture — 48,715
5. Veterans Affairs — 30,143
6. Transportation — 28,764
7. Labor — 26,274
8. Education — 23,711
9. Housing and Urban Development — 23,023
10. Energy — 13,438
11. Justice — 8,990
12. Environment (E.P.A. figure) — 5,824
13. Interior — 5,698
14. State — 4,094
15. Commerce — 2,771

*Source: Budget of The United States Government Fiscal Year 1991 page A.298. Issued by The Executive Office of the President of The United States.

Leaving Office

Whenever a member of the President's Cabinet leaves office—at the end of a President's Administration (or sooner)—the Secretary is traditionally given his leather Cabinet chair, with its brass nameplate on the back, as a memento of service. Members of the Department buy the chair for the outgoing Secretary as a parting gift.

Some Secretaries have held more than one Cabinet post over the years, and this is shown in the number of nameplates on the back of the chair. James A. Baker III has served as Chief of Staff, Secretary of Treasury, and Secretary of State; Patricia Roberts Harris as Secretary of H.U.D., H.E.W., and H.H.S. All the chairs around the Cabinet table are the same size, except the President's, which is slightly taller.

When the Cabinet meetings are over, the Secretaries return to their Departments all over Washington, while the President may go to the Oval Office to sign papers. Later, starting at 10 P.M., when many people are in bed, the entire West Wing of the White House, including the Cabinet Room, is cleaned. This is done by the General Services Administration's White House Field Office Custodial Shop. Four workers wax the floors, dust the furniture, vacuum the rugs, and polish the curatorial items. At 6 A.M. the cleaning is finished, and a new day begins at the White House.

INDEX

Numbers in *italics* refer to illustrations.